Just Do It

Just Do It

by
Buddy Harrison

HARRISON HOUSE
Tulsa, Oklahoma

Unless otherwise indicated, all Scripture quotations are taken from the *King James Version* of the Bible.

Just Do It
ISBN 0-89274-870-2
(Formerly entitled *Hear, See, Do* —
ISBN 0-89274-380-8)
Copyright © 1985, 1991 by Buddy Harrison
P. O. Box 35443
Tulsa, Oklahoma 74153

Published by Harrison House, Inc.
P. O. Box 35035
Tulsa, Oklahoma 74153

Printed in the United States of America.
All rights reserved under International Copyright Law. Contents and/or cover may not be reproduced in whole or in part in any form without the express written consent of the Publisher.

Contents

1 Think on These Things	7
2 Learning and Receiving	13
3 Two Divine Laws	17
4 Hearing, Seeing, Doing	23
5 Take Heed What You Hear	31
6 Get the Story Straight	37
7 Don't Be Dull of Hearing	47
8 Be Careful How You Hear	53
9 Cause People To Hear Joy	61
10 Catch the Vision	67

1
Think on These Things

Be careful for nothing; but in every thing by prayer and supplication with thanksgiving let your requests be made known unto God.

And the peace of God, which passeth all understanding, shall keep your hearts and minds through Christ Jesus.

Finally, brethren, whatsoever things are true, whatsoever things are honest, whatsoever things are just, whatsoever things are pure, whatsoever things are lovely, whatsoever things are of good report; if there be any virtue, and if there be any praise, think on these things.

Those things, which ye have both learned, and received, and heard, and seen in me, do: and the God of peace shall be with you.

Philippians 4:6-9

Verse 9 of this passage contains the text of our study in this book, but the entire passage provides the setting for something of importance we Christians should learn, a pattern we should follow. In verse 6 the Apostle Paul exhorts us to "be careful for nothing." In our modern-day vernacular we would express this idea by saying, "Don't get 'uptight.' Don't fret, don't be anxious." In other words, "Don't *worry*."

I wonder how many Christians know that worry is a sin. In fact, it is a much greater sin than many of the things we usually think of as being sinful — things like smoking, drinking, cursing, carousing, etc. Of course, all these things are bad. And we are right to be concerned about them and to avoid them. But actually there is a "worse" sin (if sins can be categorized as to degree). And that sin is one which is much more universally prevalent than any of the others. It is the sin of worry.

Why is worry so much worse than these other sins? For one thing, it is so widespread. Secondly, often it goes unnoticed or unchallenged; it is taken as a normal (or even a necessary) part of life. And thirdly and most importantly, worry is a killer. Worry destroys. Not just spiritually, but also mentally and physically.

But how do we know that worry is a sin? The answer is simple: The Bible says it is. In Romans 14:23 we read that **...whatsoever is not of faith is sin.** Since it is impossible to worry in faith, to engage in worry is to engage in sin. So in this passage Paul starts out by telling us not to worry. Well, if we are not supposed to worry about anything, what are we supposed to do about our problems and the situations we find ourselves in throughout our lives? Paul gives us the answer to that. We are to *pray*.

In prayer we make our requests known to God. Through prayer we petition God and receive answers and solutions from Him. If that is so, then why don't we pray more and worry less? Probably because of lack of faith. For one reason or another we either doubt that God hears our prayers or, if He does hear, that He cares enough to do anything about them.

Many people really believe that God is so big and so busy running the universe He doesn't have time to deal with their little problems. You may have felt that way yourself at times. If so, I have good news for you. The same God who spoke the world into existence and who has been operating it ever since has got ample time for His beloved children. All of them. Each of them. No request is too large or too small for Him. No heartfelt concern is ever too insignificant to warrant God's full attention.

How can we be sure of that? Again, God's own Word, the Bible, tells us so. In Matthew 10:29 our Lord Jesus tells

Think on These Things

us that not even a sparrow falls to the ground without God's knowledge. Well, if God takes note of what happens to the sparrows of this world, then surely He knows—and cares—about what happens to His own sons. (And since in Christ there is neither male nor female, we are all "sons" of God.) Once we realize that God knows and cares more about us than we even know or care about ourselves, our faith in the importance and effectiveness of our prayers will increase tremendously.

We are important to God. Vitally important. The Bible says that the very hairs of our heads are numbered. That is a great revelation. It means that every hair on our head has its own individual identification number. Whenever hair number 49 falls out, God knows it. I don't know about you, but that kind of detailed loving knowledge is enough to convince me that my heavenly Father is very much interested in me and my needs.

When I began to think about it in that light, I began to realize that my requests were not too small to take to God. I realized I can get my Father's full attention. I am important to Him. I can go to Him in confidence and receive from Him whatever it is I need. So can you. So can every one of His beloved children.

If that is so, then why do we see so many Christians still in need? The Apostle James tells us that we have not because we ask not, or because when we do ask, we "ask amiss." (James 4:2,3.) In order to receive the things we need from God, we must not only ask, we must continue to ask. We must continue to petition the Lord, placing ourselves in His capable hands. Asking Him to handle our situations and to provide the solution to them.

Then once we have "laid our burdens at the foot of the cross," we must leave them there. Why? So that "the peace of God, which passeth all understanding can keep our hearts and minds through Christ Jesus." This word "keep" means to garrison about, to guard, to protect. What is it that needs to be garrisoned about, guarded and protected? There are actually two things: the *heart* and the *mind*. YOUR heart and YOUR mind.

You see, most people think that God is just interested in the heart of man. That is just not so. God is also interested in the mind. He wants our minds affected by the Gospel as much as our hearts. He wants us to be able to think right. We know this because in the next verse of this passage, the Apostle Paul begins to deal with our thinking process.

And what is to be the pattern of our thinking? What are we told about our thoughts? **Be CAREFUL FOR NOTHING; but in every thing by PRAYER and SUPPLI-CATION with thanksgiving let your requests be made known unto God.** In other words, "Don't WORRY; ASK GOD for what you need. Turn your problems over to Him and let Him take care of them." Why? So He can answer your prayer and supplication and so His peace can garrison about, guard, protect your heart and your mind. So the peace of God can affect your thinking.

That is the trouble with most people today. They've got "stinking thinking." And they are hurt by it. As someone has said, "We Christians need to get a check-up from the neck up." That's right. It helps. It does us good. That's what Paul is saying to us here in this passage. He is telling us how to THINK. We are to fix our thoughts on "whatsoever things are true...honest...just...pure...lovely... of good report."

Now, one of the mistakes we make is taking a line or verse of scripture out of context and trying to apply it to our lives without understanding its full significance. In this passage, Paul is telling us the kinds of things we are to fix our minds upon—truth, justice, loveliness, purity, and so on. But notice that there is a little qualification added at the end of the verse. If you don't apply that qualification, you will still wind up with wrong thinking.

...if there be any virtue, and if there be any praise, think on these things. The word *virtue* literally means life. There are a lot of things in this world that are true that have no life and no praise to God in them. Isn't that so? Many things are true. The news media can inform us of how many people have been murdered and raped within the last 24 hours. And that information would be absolutely true. But that doesn't produce any life. It doesn't give any praise to God. So just because something is true does not mean that we should set our minds to think about it. Just because Sister Bucketmouth, the church gossip, repeats tales that are true, that doesn't mean that you and I need to give ear to her and to think about the things she says. Even if things are lovely, that still doesn't necessarily mean we are to think on them. It is not enough for something to be true or even beautiful to command our attention—it has got to produce virtue (life) and praise before we are to fix our mind upon it. Lovely is not good enough. Any coarse fellow on the street corner can roll his eyes as a young lady goes by and declare, "Wow! Ain't that *lovely*!" And his expressed thought might well be true. But as true as it is, as children of God we are not to fix our thoughts on such "truth."

So just because a statement qualifies on one point is not enough to qualify it as a proper subject of our attention. The things that come into the realm of our consciousness must be put to the test. They must be taken in context. They must be measured by the standard of *God's* viewpoint.

The concept Paul is expressing here is the same one he set forth in 2 Corinthians 10:5: **...bringing into CAPTIVITY every thought to the OBEDIENCE OF CHRIST.** What Paul is talking about here is nothing less than MIND CONTROL. In 1 Corinthians 2:16 he has already told us that we have **the mind of Christ.** Now he is instructing us in what to DO with that mind. And the gist of his message is this: Take CONTROL of your mind! USE it to bring life to men and glory to God!

2
Learning and Receiving

> Those things, which ye have both learned and received, and heard, and seen in me, do: and the God of peace shall be with you.
>
> Philippians 4:9

Those things, which ye have both LEARNED and RECEIVED... Notice these are two different things. Let me illustrate what I mean.

One time I went to the doctor and learned that I had bronchitis. But I decided not to receive that knowledge.

So it is possible to obtain knowledge and yet not receive it. That is what the Apostle Paul is dealing with here—getting people both to learn and to receive the things of God.

...and HEARD, and SEEN in me, DO: and the God of peace shall be with you.

Would you like to have the peace of God with you at all times? How is that accomplished? How do we assure ourselves of God's presence with us all the time? That is the message I would like to share with you in these pages.

One day while I was on a speaking tour, I had gone to my hotel room to prepare for my next speaking engagement. I had just lain down across the bed, placed my Bible on the floor, and was going over my scriptures and notes for the message I was going to deliver that evening. The scripture passage happened to be the same one I am using in this study. As I was reading these verses over, refreshing my memory, suddenly three words jumped out at me: **Hear, see, do.** At that moment revelation flowed into my heart and mind. Instantly I saw two laws of God operating in conjunction with one another in a fashion I had never seen before.

We know, of course, that God works by laws. But laws are not arbitrary. In other words, established laws are not subject to discussion or debate or argument. They aren't dependent upon individual preference. They don't change to suit public opinion. They remain in continuous effect and operate consistently and predictably without regard to human philosophy or development.

For example, suppose a person steps off the edge of the Grand Canyon or jumps out of an airplane flying at 10,000 feet. What is going to take place? Well, in accordance with the law of gravity he is going to fall. Whether he wants to or not, whether he likes it or not, whether he *believes* in gravity or not, he will fall.

Now this is where a great error has crept into the Church of Jesus Christ. Because of a misconception of God and His laws, many people have drawn some erroneous conclusions. Any time something has happened they haven't understood, they have automatically concluded it was an act of God's "sovereignty." For example, someone in the church gets sick and dies so these people conclude, "Well, it was just God's will." But the truth is, God didn't have anything to do with it. He set the law of life and death in motion and the person just allowed the death part of that law to go in motion.

For instance, suppose a person is riding a bicycle down the street. He starts to cross an intersection and fails to see an oncoming car which runs over him and kills him. Are we to automatically assume, "Oh, God took him. That was just a sovereign act of God"? No. That wasn't the law of God's sovereignty in operation; it was the law of *negligence* in operation! That death came about as a result of the law of "not looking." That was a natural consequence of a violation of the law of sight. Had the person seen the car, he would have changed his course and spared his life. It was just that simple. A natural law in operation.

Yet we Christians come along and try to put such occurrences over into a different realm. We try to spiritualize many things that don't have anything to do with the spiritual dimension. That is why we desperately need to learn to distinguish between that which is physical or natural, and that which is spiritual or supernatural. We need both to learn and to receive. And then to know what to do with what we have learned and received.

3
Two Divine Laws

In this passage from Philippians, I suddenly saw two divine laws in operation: 1) The *law of hearing*, and 2) the *law of action and reaction*.

Because it operates so dynamically, so universally, and so eternally, the divine law of hearing is probably one of the most important laws in the kingdom of God. It began to exert its influence upon you when you were still in your mother's womb. From the time of your conception, the law of hearing was in operation over you, though you were not aware of it. In fact, you still may not be fully aware of the tremendous effect of this law upon your life today.

Notice that I refer to it as *the law of* **hearing.** Now we know that Romans 10:17 says, **So then faith cometh by hearing, and hearing by the word of God.** But it is important to note that it says that faith comes by HEARING, not by HAVING HEARD. If faith came by having heard, we would only need to hear one time. That would be enough to give us faith from then on throughout the rest of our lives. But the hearing that is spoken of in this verse refers to CONTINUAL hearing.

The hearing of God's Word that produces faith is CONTINUOUS hearing. Why? Because faith is not a one-shot inoculation, not a "quick fix" which we shoot into our veins once and for all. Like manna from heaven, faith won't "keep" for very long without being used. Like our daily bread, faith is a substance which must be continually replenished.

Faith is not an inanimate object like a stone or a staff; it is a living organism. Faith is alive, it is growing, it is constantly maturing. Like our physical bodies, faith must be fed and nurtured and exercised; otherwise, it becomes weak and eventually dies.

But how do we "feed" our faith? What is "faith food"? The Apostle Paul tells us it is the Word of God. But why does Paul specify that the God-kind of faith comes by hearing *God's* words? Because natural human faith comes by hearing man's words just as negative or evil faith (fear) comes by hearing Satan's words.

So this law of hearing is much broader than most Christians have realized. In 1 Corinthians 14:10 Paul writes: **There are, it may be, so many kinds of voices in the world, and none of them is without signification.** Today we certainly know there are lots of voices, don't we? If nothing else, we have the media: radio, television, newspapers, magazines, books. All these things are constantly saying something to us. They represent "voices" which are continually speaking to us. And, as Paul notes, these voices are not without significance, which means they do have meaning. Much of what they say is true, humanly speaking.

But what about the spirit realm? Does Satan speak? Do the demons have voices? Of course. What about God? Does He speak to us? What about Jesus? And the Holy Spirit? How about the angels, the **ministering spirits, sent forth to minister for them who shall be heirs of salvation** (Heb. 1:14)? Yes, glory be to God, they all speak!

And in the natural realm we have all kinds of people who are speaking to us all the time. Our fellow workers on the job. Friends. Neighbors. Relatives. Family members. All of these people have voices. And they use them.

What about within our own selves? Does our own spirit speak to us? How about our mind, does it talk to us? And our body? (If you don't think your body speaks to you, just

Two Divine Laws

go on a three-day fast and see how quickly it begins to talk to you—loud and clear!)

There are many voices in our realm of existence. The law of hearing is already at work in us producing that which we continually hear, whether it comes from the outside or the inside. This is one of the things I saw in this passage. The operation and effect of the law of hearing.

This explains why Moslems have been so successful in establishing all of their children in their faith and keeping them as faithful Moslems: they make maximum utilization of the law of hearing. From the time a child is born into that society, even while it is still nursing at its mother's breast, all those around it are continually whispering in its ear, "Mohammed is God, Mohammed is God, Mohammed is God."

We want to operate the law of hearing on the positive side and make it work for us rather than against us. The law of hearing is an integral part of determining who and what we are.

The second law — of action and reaction — actually comes from 2 Corinthians 9:6-8. Most of us know it as the law of sowing and reaping: **...whatsoever a man soweth, that shall he also reap** (Gal. 6:7). And, **...with what measure ye mete, it shall be measured to you again** (Matt. 7:2). But it too applies to a much broader base than what we have seen. The basic law of physics is: For every action there is a separate and equal reaction. Expressed in spiritual terms, it would be: As you purpose in your heart to act, so you determine the reaction you will receive.

I learned this principle when the Lord said to me, "Son, you can take the same action with a different purpose, enter it into your heart, and thus produce a different reaction." And He gave me this example. He said, "If you take a pebble and carelessly toss it into the water, it will produce

19

a small series of ripples. But if you purpose differently in your heart, if you purposefully take a big rock and throw it accurately and energetically, you will produce a much greater and more powerful reaction."

You see, the governing factor is what is purposed in the heart. I began to see that *purpose* is the key to *production*. That is the theoretical aspect of the principle. Actually I had to learn the practical application of it the hard way.

Since I own a religious publishing house, I deal with a lot of Christian people, especially ministers who want their manuscripts published. One of the preachers I dealt with several times was always wanting a better deal than what was offered him. (Have you ever met anyone like that?) He was never satisfied. It didn't matter how fair the terms were, he always wanted more generous ones. And one of the main arguments he used on me was, "Remember now, I'm a brother."

Finally that line got to where it irked me to no end. But he was persistent. He was one of those pushy people who just won't take no for an answer. He kept constantly pushing and badgering and staying after me until he wore me down.

At first I would say, "No, those are my terms." And he would immediately start in on me to do better. After so long I would say, "All right, all right, you win. I'm going to plant a seed in your ministry." And I would go ahead and give the man the terms he wanted.

This had gone on for some time. Finally one day I was in need of a return on my investment in his ministry. And, of course, when you need to reap a little of what you have been sowing, naturally you go first to the Lord. So I started in on God about my return. I began praying, "Now, Lord, I have planted seed in this man's ministry—lots of seed. He and I have developed a very close relationship, an

Two Divine Laws

intimate relationship, in fact—his hand is firmly implanted in my back pocket! I have been sowing for quite a while now, and I need to start reaping some of what I've been sowing. So I am expecting a return right now."

That was the truth. I was expecting a big return from this fellow because I had invested a lot of money in his ministry. Then the Spirit of the Lord spoke up on the inside of me. "Son," he said, "you obviously don't know the difference between giving and giving in."

I was surprised, and confused. "What do you mean?" I asked.

"The governing factor of that law I taught you is, 'as you purpose in your heart,' " He said. "You purposed in your heart to shut that man up and get him off your back. The law worked. That's what you purposed to accomplish, so that's what you got."

Right then I learned a hard, but very valuable lesson. It's not what we do that counts as much as WHY we are doing it! That lesson made me much more careful about my seed planting. I learned to sow with a purpose.

You see, we need to plant with the right attitude. The scripture tells us that God loves what kind of a giver? Fearful? No, cheerful. God loves a *cheerful* giver. (2 Cor. 9:7.) It does make a difference HOW we give.

What we must understand is this: If we work the law the right way, it will bless us. If we work it the wrong way, it will curse us.

These two divine laws work in conjunction with each other. Together they will produce for us anything we need for successful Christian living. But they must be fully understood and intelligently applied. Otherwise they will backfire and produce the very opposite of what we desire. This is why so many Christians are failing and, often as not, laying the blame for their failure on God.

Just Do It

If these divine laws do not seem to be working in your life, I can assure you the fault is not God's. If your Christian life is not all you would like it to be, perhaps you need to take a closer look at these laws and how you have been applying them in your own life. Properly understood and applied, God's divine laws work!

4
Hearing, Seeing, Doing

I find the comedian, Flip Wilson, very amusing. One of his famous lines is: "What you see is what you get." I would like to paraphrase that statement a little bit in order to combine the two laws of hearing and action-reaction into one: *What you hear is what you see, and what you see is what you will do.* That is divine law.

That law is in operation all the time. Whether you realize it or not, it is going to work over you all the days of your life. It started when you were in your mother's womb and will work all the way through until the end. And if you don't understand the operation of that divine law, it will bring curses upon you. But if you do understand it, you can make it work for you to bless you, to produce for you that which you need and desire. That is what I want to share with you in this book: How to recognize, understand and use this divine law of hearing, seeing, doing — and use it not only for yourself, but for all those around you.

When I first became aware of this law and its operation, I began to think back over my life to see how it had affected me personally. I recalled several instances which seemed to prove its validity in my own life.

For example, I remembered the time when my wife and I were first married and I was working for a truck line loading freight out on the dock. I had gotten in good with the dock foreman so I could pretty well "call the shots" when it came to working conditions.

Within reason, I could decide the hours I wanted to work. I could take a break when I felt I needed one without having to ask permission. If I needed to take a day off for some reason, all I had to do was call in and inform the foreman and it would be taken care of. Everything was great. I had it made.

But then things began to change. Rumors (what the army calls "scuttlebutt") began to trickle down through the company. Soon the tales were flying hard and fast. We heard we were going to get a new dock foreman and that he was a real "toughy." We heard how mean and nasty he was and how rough he was going to make it on all of us. This fellow did everything "right by the book," supposedly, and was such a stickler for discipline and order that we wouldn't even be able to go to the restroom without getting permission!

Over and over again for two weeks I heard all those stories about the new foreman. And for two weeks I was busy painting a mental picture of this ornery cuss. The first day I saw that man set foot on the dock, I took one look at him and thought to myself, "Now there is a fat head if I ever saw one!"

Why? Because the law of hearing had already started operating within me. What I had heard and heard about him had engraved an image in my mind of what he was like before I had ever even met the man.

Have you ever formed an opinion of someone before you ever even met them? If so, that law of hearing was operating on you, and you didn't even know it. You weren't even aware of it. Why did it work so well on you? Because words paint pictures. If you had heard different words, you might well have formed a different mental picture. But as a result of what you had heard, you formed an opinion of someone without ever knowing the facts about them.

That applies to all of us. We form opinions based on what we have been told, rather than what we have experienced, on what we have *heard* rather than what we *know* to be true. How important it is that we be careful what we hear!

Then I began to recall another instance of how this law had worked on me. This one was farther back to when I was still in high school. (In fact, the farther back I went, the more I saw.)

During my junior year in high school, I had the glorious privilege of being the tallest player on our basketball team. I was all of five feet, eleven inches tall. So I really had to work at it to play ball against the other teams whose players were usually at least six feet tall, some even six-four, six-six, and six-eight. But because I was the tallest on our team, I was chosen as center. This meant I had to jump center court against these giants. I also had to guard them the whole ball game, which was no easy task.

But I managed to hold my own. Until we came up against a team whose center and tallest player was seven feet tall! All of a sudden I began to feel woefully inadequate. I could identify with the Israeli spies who came back from the land of Canaan declaring that compared to the giants of Canaan they were as grasshoppers in their own eyes!

But, of course, the team coaches were well aware of the situation and my need for a little dose of self-confidence, so they started getting me ready for the big game. Besides the usual game plan strategy, they began to work on my self-image. They started telling me, "Harrison, don't worry about this guy. You can take him. He's tall, sure, but he's slow, real slow. You're fast, you're quick. Why, when the official tosses up that ball, you'll leave that guy standing flat-footed!"

"Not only that," they told me, "you can run circles around him out on the court. You'll have him bushed just trying to keep up with you out there."

They started painting a mental picture for me. They were getting me in the right frame of mind, building my image of myself, getting me to see myself as a winner. They told me that this fellow was so used to outjumping people easily that he had gotten lax.

"He just kind of lifts up on his tiptoes and slaps at the ball," they told me. "You can go up real quick and take him every time." They kept insisting that if I would be alert and quick, I could take the other guy with no problem. I would be the hero of the game.

"Go get him, Harrison! Take him! Outjump him! Outrun him! Outscore him!"

After a while it began to work. I started to halfway believe it. I got a piece of chalk, went out in the gym, and started jumping. Every time I jumped, I made a mark on the gym wall. Then I would go to work to see if I couldn't beat my own record. All week long I worked at it.

All the while I was jumping I was planning my strategy, figuring my moves, plotting how I was going to "take this dude." Not just the first jump, but all the way through the game. And the more I worked and planned and figured and plotted, the more I saw myself actually pulling it off.

Finally it came time for the big game. I was so fired up I could hardly hold myself back. During the warmup period I jumped higher than ever and made shots I had never made before in my life. I was ready! I could hardly wait to get onto that court and take that guy!

But then I looked down the court and saw the opposing player for the first time. He looked to me like a walking tree! And the closer he got to me, the taller that tree grew! By the time we faced each other in the center of the court, he looked like a giant redwood! For a moment, I almost lost my mental image. But then what I had heard all that time came rushing back into my mind: "Sure he's tall, but you can take him! You can take him! You can take him!"

So I just got set, took a deep breath, and turned all my attention to that ball. When the official tossed it up into the air, up I went with it. Do you know what happened? First crack out of the box, I outjumped that guy! And from then on, the psychological advantage was all mine. Why? Because the law of hearing, seeing, doing was in operation. It worked!

I see this principle at work in my church, because what people are hearing about it is the picture they have of it. Before they ever attend a service there, before they ever even lay eyes on the church, they have an image in their minds of what it is like. Whatever my people go out and say about the church is the picture that is painted for the rest of the city.

We have learned to operate that law of hearing over other people. It works *for* us instead of against us. We have learned that if we keep on saying good things, we produce good things. But if we say bad things, that is what we receive.

I saw this principle work when we first started out meeting in the back of an office building. We were there for a couple of months, then we went over to a high school auditorium for another couple of months. It was coming up summertime and since there was no air conditioning in the high school, we went out looking for another place to meet. Finally we located a building that had been used as a flea market. It had all kinds of little shops in it, all painted up in bright colors with pretty handmade signs hung everywhere. So we just gutted one side of the building and made it into an auditorium. On the other side we left the shops to serve as classrooms for the church. It was so cheery, so bright and colorful with all those reds, greens, and yellows everywhere.

It wasn't long before we could tell who the visitors in our services had been listening to and the mental picture they had painted of us because we came to be known as "the wild bunch." Now our congregation does like to worship God freely. We sing, shout, dance, clap, run around — you name it. With that kind of reputation, we knew what to expect when new people came to visit. The moment they set foot in the church vestibule, they would take one look at all those colorful banners and exclaim, "I knew it — a circus!" Why? Because they saw what they were *expecting* to see, what they had been *told* to expect to see. What they heard is what they saw.

But I have also seen that law work positively for us. When people go out talking about the love and the power of God that is in our midst and how precious the people are in our fellowship, that is what is produced. When people walk into our building, it's not long before the love of God just overwhelms them. That is one reason people can go there and get healed. They EXPECT to find healing there, and so they do.

For example, one time I was preaching on the radio and a little old lady from a very conservative denominational church heard me. This lady had suffered for many years from arthritis in her knees. She had been taught all of her life by her church not to expect to be made well because it was not always God's will to heal.

But then she heard me preaching the healing message of God's great love. The more she listened, the more she believed it. And the more she believed it, the more she became convinced that if she could just somehow get to our church, she would be healed of her crippling arthritis.

Finally she got up enough courage and strength to make her way to the church. On that particular Sunday the hostess at the entrance was a certain black lady from our congregation who just loves to stand by the door and worship and praise God with all her being. She was dancing around and singing and making a joyful noise unto the Lord, when suddenly the Spirit of God spoke to her and told her to dance with the next person who walked through the door.

Wouldn't you know it? About that time, in walked the little old lady with arthritis. But the black sister didn't know about this lady's condition; she just knew she was supposed to dance with the next person who entered the church. And so she did.

She rushed over to the little old lady, threw her arms around her, and hugged her warmly, exclaiming, "Praise the Lord, Honey, glory to God." And then she dragged her off dancing in the Spirit! And the little old lady was instantly healed!

Why? Because God moved in the supernatural realm to bring to pass just what the little old lady had envisioned in her heart and mind. She had heard herself say over and over, "If I can just get to that church, I will be healed." And so she was! The law worked!

That law will work for you, too, if you allow it to. Why? Because words paint pictures. And what we continually and consistently picture in our hearts and minds has a way of becoming reality.

If that is so, that means that you and I have the power to create our own world by the mental image we create when we speak forth with our mouths. When we speak something out, it runs right back around into our own ears and enters our minds and hearts to produce a picture. And that picture, held firmly enough and long enough, will eventually reproduce itself in the physical realm: *"What you see* (in your mind) *is what you get* (in your world)."

The reason we confess the Word of God is so that we can form God's own image and build God's world. By faith and confession of the Word of God, we utilize that law to make it work for us. By believing God's Word in our heart and speaking it forth out of our mouth, we create an image in our minds which produces the physical manifestation in our world.

You and I are cocreators with God. And the law we use to create is the divine law of hearing, seeing, doing!

5
Take Heed What You Hear

In Psalm 119:130 the Psalmist says of the Lord, **The entrance of thy words giveth light; it giveth understanding unto the simple.** "The entrance of thy word giveth light..." Now if you thought about this statement in the natural, wouldn't you think the entrance of God's Word would bring *sound*? But according to this scripture it doesn't. It brings *light*. It causes a person to see. What you HEAR is what you SEE. Words paint pictures.

In Mark 4:23 the Lord Jesus told the people of His day, **If any man have ears to hear, let him hear.** It sounds to me like some people who have ears still don't hear — that a lot of people are deaf, or just don't really listen. They tune out. That is certainly true.

Then in verse 24 we read: **And he said unto them, Take heed what ye hear: with what measure ye mete, it shall be measured to you: and unto you that hear shall more be given.** "Take heed what ye hear." Notice that this is a command. Usually the understood subject of an imperative sentence like this is the pronoun you: "You take heed what you hear." This means that the responsibility is upon YOU to take heed what YOU hear. In other words, you can control the content of what goes into you. That means that you have the freedom, the duty, the power either to accept or to reject what comes into your realm of consciousness. That means you can tune it out if it is not edifying.

Now this will tell you why God is dealing so strongly today with things like gossip. What is wrong with gossip?

It is a perversion of the basic law of hearing. It is receiving the negative, the bad, the evil side of any situation. And once a person starts to do that, he begins to plant the seeds of his own destruction. That's why God is against gossip. Because it is harmful. Not just to the injured party, the person who is talked about, but also to the hearer, the one who receives the negative message into his ear and mind and heart. That is why the Bible teaches us to let our nay be nay and our yea be yea. (Matt. 5:37.)

The Lord is telling us to guard our spirits: "Don't confuse your spirit. Don't operate the law to your own detriment. Because what you hear is what you will see. And what you see is what you will get. Take heed how you hear!"

The computer world has a term: *GIGO*. It means, "Garbage In, Garbage Out." In other words, what you put into the computer system is precisely what you will get out of it.

There is a lot of garbage in this world. And it is not all confined to the secular world. Some of it is passed off on us as being "Christian." There are things in the media which disguise themselves as "Christian" but are not that at all. Yet most believers don't seem to be able, or care enough, to examine them for what they really are.

Just because something is aired on a Christian radio or television station does not necessarily mean that you and I should listen to it. Certainly not day in and day out. We need to be more selective, more discriminative about what we allow into our ears. Because what goes in our ears goes into our minds and hearts. It becomes part of us.

As Christians, it is our responsibility to observe this divine law and make it work for us rather than become a curse against us. Unless you determine in your heart to take heed to what you hear, it won't be done. Because there is

Take Heed What You Hear

no one else who can do it for you. No one else is responsible for you but you.

Be careful who and what you listen to. Examine the content of what comes into your mind. Know what is going in, whether it is truth or garbage. You know, there are some people who will use your ears as garbage dumps if you let them. It will be like backing up a garbage truck to your back door and dumping garbage all over your yard.

Have you ever wondered why you feel dirty after some people have finished talking to you? You feel dirty because they have just dumped THEIR garbage all over you. And you let them. You shouldn't do that. Garbage pollutes. It affects your spirit and your thinking. That law has been working the wrong way on you.

When such people start in on you like that, you have an obligation to refuse to receive what they are putting out. Now that doesn't mean you have to be nasty or obnoxious about it. That doesn't mean you are to embarrass people or put them down. You don't have to throw the garbage back in their face. That wouldn't be Christian anyway. It just means that you don't have to receive what they put out. It means you need to be careful to guard and protect your own ears.

You are to take heed to what you hear, and to the people you listen to. That is a command. If you don't protect your hearing, it will affect your faith. Then you will wonder why you are having such a hard time maintaining a high faith level. Here you are believing God for healing and Aunt Susie is saying, "Why, you know, you can't ever tell if God will heal or not." You don't need to slap Aunt Susie across the mouth and order her to shut up! But you do need to tune her out.

Right then you need to take heed to what you are hearing. And that doesn't mean to take a superior, know-it-all attitude and stance. Exercising care over your hearing doesn't mean that you act like you are better or more spiritual than Aunt Susie. It just means you take responsibility for what goes into your mind and heart.

For he that hath, to him shall be given: and he that hath not, from him shall be taken even that which he hath (Mark 4:25). That may sound confusing. Let's put it into modern-day vernacular: The value a person places upon what he hears is the value he will get out of it. If you place great value upon what you hear, you will derive great value from it. If you place little value upon it, you will get little value from it. The entrance of God's Word (His wisdom and knowledge) gives light. And the more we open ourselves to receive that Word, the more light we are given. The more light, the greater the revelation. It just goes on and on.

But the opposite is also true. If we place little value upon God's Word, then we will get little or nothing out of it. In fact, we will begin to lose even the revelation we have already received: **For whosoever hath, to him shall be given . . . but whosoever hath not, from him shall be taken away even that he hath** (Matt. 13:12).

As a Christian, you have got to take heed what you hear. But you also have to determine the real value of it.

For example, if what you are reading right now is a message from God, and if you receive it as such, then you will receive more and more revelation from it as you read. However, if it is a message from God and you refuse to accept or receive it as such, then you won't get anything out of what is being presented. Not only that, but you will lose some revelation that you have already received. Take heed WHAT you hear. And HOW you hear it. And what VALUE you place upon it. When you listen, attitude is as important as attentiveness.

Luke, recording this same teaching from the Lord, states it this way: **Take heed therefore** *how* **ye hear: for** whosoever hath, to him shall be given; and whosoever hath not, from him shall be taken even that which he *seemeth* to have (Luke 8:18). In the *King James Version* the columnar note reads: **Or, thinketh that he hath.**

Mark says, **Take heed WHAT you hear.** The emphasis is on CONTENT. Luke says, **Take heed HOW you hear.** The emphasis is on ATTITUDE.

Attitude can affect hearing. If a person approaches the Gospel with an open mind and heart, he will receive the truth that is contained in it. If he approaches it with a closed mind and heart, then as far as he is concerned there is no truth in it to receive. His attitude cuts him off from the revelation that is there. In fact, Scripture tells us that he will lose even what understanding he *seems* to already have, or what he *thinks he has*.

That explains why some people have gone in the direction they have and why their lives are in the state they are in. It isn't because they didn't hear the content of the message: it's because of their wrong attitude in listening. And with the wrong attitude even the very Word of God will roll off them like water off a duck's back. It will never penetrate them, never affect them, never change them.

It is not enough to go to church or to listen to the Gospel or to read the Bible. All these things represent content. There has also got to be a certain amount of "want to" involved. There must be a DESIRE to receive as well as a willingness to listen.

We want people to keep going to church and listening to the Gospel and reading the Bible even though they may not really want to do so.

We know that if they keep at it long enough, eventually the Spirit of the Lord will move upon their minds and hearts and bring revelation. But unless and until their heart is opened to receive that Spirit of truth, they will listen and listen and never really hear. Why? Because they don't really

Just Do It

WANT to hear. The key is ATTITUDE. Ultimately people hear what they want to hear.

That's why we are told to take heed HOW we hear. Because we hear what we WANT to hear.

6
Get the Story Straight

What you hear and how you hear it is important. Unless you pay careful attention to both, you won't get the story straight. You won't hear everything. You will hear only a part, only pieces. You'll actually hear things in reverse, like those children who suffer from the physical disease which causes them to hear words backwards. I believe there are many people who do the same thing spiritually. They are spiritually deformed so they don't hear things right.

I know of one particular lady who loved the ministry and message of Kenneth Hagin. She used to come to every one of his seminars and sit on the front row where she could soak up every word that fell from his lips. Since she taught a college and career class in Sunday school back in her own denominational church, she would go back on Sunday morning and try to teach Brother Hagin's material to her class. But she would invariably get up and quote just the opposite of what Brother Hagin had said.

The pastor of that church heard about what she was teaching and became quite disturbed about it. Finally he called me to find out what was going on.

"Say, what does this fellow Hagin believe anyway?" he asked me, obviously upset.

"What do you mean?" I replied.

Then the pastor began to tell me some of the things this lady was saying she had gotten from listening to Brother Hagin. It was the exact opposite of what he had been teaching. What was the problem? The lady was well intentioned, but she just didn't hear right.

Every preacher has to contend with this sort of thing. He knows that in every congregation there will be those who will listen very politely, then go out and "repeat" things he never said or meant to say. Why does that happen? Why do people mishear so badly? Because of their wrong attitude. If the attitude is wrong, the message will come through all wrong.

Words paint pictures. But what picture they paint depends not only on the speaker but also on the listener. Unless we listen very carefully we can get a fragmented or jumbled or distorted picture. Like a television transmission, the picture is only as good as the receiver. In this case, the receiver is in the head of the listener. The picture is received through the ears and is projected onto the mind. But if our ears (our receivers) are not tuned correctly, then our minds receive a faulty image.

Do you know why some people never get filled with the Holy Spirit? They have never heard enough words to produce the correct image in their minds and hearts.

Do you know why some people never get healed? Because they have simply never gotten the picture. They have never seen that sickness in their body, never seen the Lord Jesus walk down inside them, take up that disease, bear it on His own back, and walk away with it. If they could ever get that picture down on the inside of them, they would realize, "Glory to God, it's gone. I don't have it anymore. I'm healed!" And they would be.

Words paint pictures. Many people are constantly in turmoil because we Christians have painted the wrong picture for them. We have not instructed them in line with the Word of God.

People want to receive the Holy Ghost. And we give them confusing and contradictory word pictures. We paint them the wrong image, and get them doing the wrong thing. This happens all because somebody is saying words to them, utilizing that law over them incorrectly, giving them the wrong mental picture. Because of this they go about trying to receive in the wrong way. And neither of us understands why it isn't "working."

I know this from my own experience. I can remember when I came forward at age eleven to receive the Holy Spirit. I had been hearing people talk and preach about the Holy Ghost and speaking in tongues and all that, so finally one day a friend and I decided that, bless God, we were going to go down to the front of the church and "get the Holy Ghost."

But when we went forward in a revival service to receive this marvelous gift we had heard so much about, we found out it wasn't nearly as easy as we had been led to believe. All of a sudden we found ourselves surrounded, besieged by a crowd of well-meaning but over-zealous church members who seemed to be talking at once and telling us all kinds of bewildering and confusing things to do in order to receive.

One of these "counselors" grabbed my arms and held them like a vise, while somebody else was busy slapping me on the back and urging me to "turn loose, son, turn loose!" I didn't know what he was talking about. I didn't have hold of anything; at least, not that I knew of.

While I was trying to figure out what he was getting at, the rest of them started in on me with all of their different gimmicks. One was telling me to say glory as fast as I could. So I did. Now you can't say glory very many times very fast without getting your tongue all tangled up. When that happened, they all got real worked up and started blabbing excitedly, "That's it, that's it! Let the Holy Ghost speak!" So I did. I shut up and gave the Holy Ghost a chance to speak His piece. But He didn't say a thing.

Just Do It

You see, at every stage of the game, I did just what they told me to do. And I got nothing. The law was in operation. These folks meant well, I'm sure, but what were they doing wrong? They were painting a picture with their words. But the image they were painting was just confusing me. They really didn't know how to use their words to properly instruct me in how to go about receiving the Spirit and allowing Him to speak *through* me. I was expecting something entirely different to happen, because I had the wrong mental picture of what was *supposed* to happen and how it was to take place.

You see, those people didn't tell me that it was not the Holy Ghost but the disciples who spoke in tongues that day at Pentecost. The Bible says, ...*they* **were all filled with the Holy Ghost, and** (they) **began to speak with other tongues, as the Spirit gave** *them* **utterance** (Acts 2:4). The disciples did the talking, not the Holy Spirit. The Spirit just gave them the urge. They were the ones who spoke it forth.

Speaking in tongues is part natural and part divine. The natural part is us doing the talking. The divine part is what is being said to God. It is up to us to speak the sounds that come to our lips. It is up to the Holy Spirit to make a language out of those sounds and it is easy to receive when you get the right instructions.

But these people didn't give me that picture. I got the wrong one. I was trying to let the Holy Ghost do the talking. I was waiting for Him to speak. As a result, I was struggling to get the Holy Ghost and just couldn't seem to be able to do it. Why? Because somebody had painted the wrong image of how the Spirit is received.

But, bless their hearts, they didn't give up. They wouldn't let me go until I got what I had come for. They beat on me and pulled on me and hovered over me until I thought I was going to expire right there! One even stood in front of me and spit on me! (That'll bless you!)

Get the Story Straight

By that time I was no more conscious of spiritual things than a drunken sailor. I was sweating and trembling. My legs were aching, my knees were hurting, and my toes had curled under three times. I was in a daze and ready to give it all up as a lost cause.

I was tired, frustrated,—and irritated. I had come down front in all honesty and simplicity to receive this marvelous gift and there I was being manhandled like I had come to steal something! I hadn't done anything wrong. I just wanted to get the Holy Spirit I had heard so much about.

These people had talked about it, preached about it, sung about it. I had been told repeatedly that it was a free gift and that I ought to have it. I had been urged time and time again to come receive it. Then when I came to get it, it seemed to me like everybody and his brother had jumped all over me. I couldn't understand this at all!

I was really struggling just to keep my sanity. By then all I wanted was just to get out of there as quickly as I could. But the way was blocked. I was caught. On top of all that, whoever was in front of me had the most ungodly breath I had ever smelled in my life. It was positively nauseous. So there I was, trying to pray, and all I could think of was how putrid that guy's mouth was! This was not exactly the height of spiritual attunement!

You see, those dear people were sincere, but ignorant. They were going about this thing all wrong simply because they did not know how to use words to paint the proper picture. They didn't know how to use language to create an image.

Finally it just became too much for me. Out of sheer frustration and embarrassment I suddenly burst into tears. As I was crying, my lips were quivering.

Realizing that the Bible says that with "stammering lips" God would speak to His people, my grandfather got up from his place and came down to the front to stand by my side. Kindly and without great emotion, he pointed his finger at me and said, "That's it, sonny boy; that's the Holy Ghost helping you. Just go ahead and speak that out." The moment he said that, I saw it. I just let go and began to speak in other tongues.

Why? What had happened? The law had first been incorrectly applied and had worked against me. Then it was used properly and worked for me.

This kind of thing happens all the time. We just haven't always recognized it as such. This is what happens so much of the time when people have difficulty getting saved, or healed, or filled with the Spirit, because other people are operating that law erroneously over them. They drive them farther away from their goal rather than closer to it.

The ones who come for salvation or healing or the infilling of the Spirit often get the wrong picture. They hear the wrong things, and therefore, get the wrong mental image. As a result, they never receive what they were really after. Because they hear wrong, they see wrong, and do wrong.

That also tells us why it is so important that we speak good words over our children. Have you ever wondered why so many of our children today turn out the way they do? I can tell you why. It's because of what they have been hearing at home, in church, at school.

That's why Christian schools have become so important to us: not so we can save our children from the world, but so we can have them under our supervision in order to work the law of hearing on them. That way we can make it work for us and them rather than against us both so what they are constantly hearing at school lines up with what they are hearing at home and in church.

We are not on the defensive — not running scared. We simply understand the law that what you hear is what you see, and that if you don't hear it right, you won't see it right. And if you don't see right, you won't do right.

As a kid growing up, I was constantly being told, "You're sorry, you're just no good, you'll never amount to anything."

I heard that. I saw that. I went out and lived that. That's where I was headed until a certain man came into my life. When I married his daughter, he surrounded me with love and faith. He spoke the Word of God over me. He told me, "Buddy, you can accomplish anything you want to in this life. You can do all things through Christ who strengthens you. You are more than a conqueror."

"Who me?" I asked.

That's not the image I had of myself in my mind and heart. So I had to keep hearing that message over and over again. It was like an artist painting a fine portrait, and he had to keep applying successive brush strokes, one over the other, gradually bringing forth the image he wanted to portray in my innermost being.

That's what you and I are to do. Use our tongues to create. We should be able to say with the Psalmist David: **My tongue is the pen of a ready writer** (Ps. 45:1).

We need to just keep speaking forth the Word of God over ourselves, our family members, our pastor and fellow church members; in fact, over everyone we associate with. We need to constantly be putting that picture in them, painting a portrait of them, building an image in them: "You are wonderful. You are good. You can do it. You are an overcomer, an achiever, more than a conqueror."

Once I saw what a tremendous effect that law had upon my own outlook and life, I began to apply it to my own family. I never had the trouble with my children that other people seemed to have with theirs. I have three marvelous children — two girls and a boy. The most trouble I ever had with any of my children was with my youngest daughter, Cookie. And that didn't last very long.

Once for about six months Cookie got it into her head she wanted to be a little rebellious. She thought she wanted to try the way of the world, to do a few things her way. So she started trying it. At the end of the school year, she decided she wanted to take part in some school activities that her mother and I really didn't care for. So we laid down some rules about what she could do, where she could go, and what time she had to be home.

One time Cookie went out and didn't come back on time. Naturally, her mother and I were concerned about her. So I began to pray to make sure that everything was all right. As I was praying, the Lord revealed to me where Cookie was, who she was with, and what she was doing. When Cookie walked in a couple of hours later, her mother asked her where she'd been. She assured her mother that she'd gone where she was supposed to go but that she'd just been unavoidably delayed.

I knew better. I said, "Hold it a minute, Cookie. Before you say anything else, before you get into trouble, let me tell you where you went, who you were with, and what you did." And I did. After that, Cookie was never rebellious again.

Why? Because right then a picture was painted in her heart and mind. She saw right away that she was never going to be able to get away with anything. She realized she might as well straighten up and do right because Daddy was always going to know about her activities. And Daddy always did.

You see, you can run your household by the Holy Ghost. You can raise your children by the Holy Spirit. And it will be effective.

So I began to think about this law: how it had worked on me all my life, how people had affected me through the years. I thought about the ones who had helped me and the ones who had caused me to struggle. And I asked myself why. I realized it was because of what they had said that had painted a picture in my mind at the time. That's why it is so important to be careful who you listen to and how you listen.

There will always be those who listen to the wrong people and those who don't listen at all. And there will be those who don't get the story straight when they do listen.

I get amused with Charles Capps who tells a funny story about how he was 18 years old before he ever got the courage to play the game of marbles. Being from Arkansas (where everybody is supposed to be a hillbilly), Charles said that the people he grew up with called that game "marvels." So the reason it took him so long to get the courage to play it was because he had heard all his life in church that Jesus gave an injunction, "Marvel not." So he didn't!

But as amusing as that little story is, there is a lot of truth in it. People are still hearing things wrong and drawing from them all kinds of silly doctrines. That's exactly where strange doctrines spring from: from somebody's not hearing right. That's how that law gets perverted so that it produces error rather than truth, a curse rather than a blessing.

Have you ever noticed how some people can listen to you explain something very carefully and still get a totally different meaning out of your message than what you were actually trying to say? They hear the words all right, but they don't really hear what you say. That happens to all of us. As one speaker once told his audience, "Don't listen to what I say; listen to what I *mean*." Some people hear everything that is said; they just can't seem to hear what is meant.

I like the story of the little boy in Sunday school who heard his teacher tell about how Lot's wife looked back and turned into a pillar of salt. He was quick to interject, "Aw, Teacher, that's nothin'. Once when my mama was driving down the street, she looked back and turned into a telephone pole!" He heard the words all right — he just didn't quite get the message.

There are thousands of people sitting in our churches today who are like that little boy. They hear the right words, but somehow never get the right meaning. And because they don't hear right, they don't see right, so they don't do right. That law is in operation over them. And the worst part is, most of them never realize what is wrong, where they are missing it, or why they are having (and causing!) so much trouble.

It is vitally important to get the message clear, to get it accurate, to be certain we have heard right. What has happened in the Church is that we have seen things that weren't there and missed the things that were there. It is not enough just to hear. It is not even enough to listen to the right people. We also need to be very careful to get the story straight!

7
Don't Be Dull of Hearing

In Hebrews 5:11 the writer tells the Jewish believers, **...we have many things to say** (to you), **and hard to be uttered, seeing ye are** *dull of hearing*. These words insinuate that the Children of Israel were not allowed to enter the Promised Land the first time because they were "dull of hearing."

I pray God that this scripture does not describe you. If you are not enjoying health, prosperity, success, peace, happiness, and contentment—the fruit of God's blessing—it may be because you are dull of hearing.

I am not trying to offend you, only to call attention to the fact that there is a reason why people miss out on God's best. Many times it is simply because of faulty hearing, because this law does work. What you hear does have a great deal to do with what you see and what you get in life. As a Christian, you have to understand this law and get it to work for you so it can bless you. Otherwise, it is going to work against you. You need to be careful how you hear.

My youngest daughter Cookie is one of those happy-go-lucky people. She's easygoing and extroverted, the type who never meets a stranger. As a child growing up, she spent half her time in "La La Land"—in her own little world. Therefore, she only heard half of what was said to her and less of what was going on around her. As a result, you never knew what was going to come out of Cookie's mouth.

Just Do It

One time I was called to Minnesota to serve as music and youth director of a church. During the time I was there, I was up directing the choir while my wife was singing in the choir. Our girls were about five and six years old then, so I would sit them on the front row where we could watch them. They were generally well behaved. I only had to correct them twice during the entire 16 months we were there. But they did do a lot of giggling to themselves, and I knew why. Cookie was always getting her words mixed up and coming out with funny remarks.

The fact is, Cookie just couldn't talk plain. So my other daughter Candy would sometimes try to get her to repeat things just to hear how she would garble them up. But the reason Cookie had such a hard time saying things right was because she never heard them right.

Songs that you and I know and understand came out a little different when Cookie sang them. For example, her favorite church hymn was "Amazing *Grapes*"! She loved that song.

I used to wonder to myself, "The way Cookie hears, how does she see God? I really wonder how she pictures the Lord." While the rest of us were singing the chorus from "Victory in Jesus" ("He sought me, and He bought me"), Cookie was loudly proclaiming for all to hear, "He sought me, and He *bit* me!"

"Surely," I told myself, "such a child cannot have a good image of God. It's just not possible."

But I think the classic example of how Cookie misheard and, therefore, misquoted was the time Brother Hagin heard her singing at the top of her voice what he recognized as a line from the spiritual song entitled "All My Sin's Been Taken Away." The line was supposed to declare positively, "My Lord has done just what He said." But Cookie's version was: "My Lord's so sick, He can't raise His head!"

Don't Be Dull of Hearing

Now I ask you, what kind of an image could she have of her Lord if that was the way she saw Him? How could she believe God for healing when she saw Him "as sick as a dog" Himself?

We laugh at things like that, and they are amusing. Kids do get funny ideas sometimes. And I'm sure that our Father sometimes gets a good laugh at some of the things He hears us say. Like kids, we don't always hear accurately. And as a result, we wind up with a not-so-clear view of things, many times with a perverted view. We get things all tangled up, all twisted. We get a distorted view of God, of ourselves, and of life in general.

I'm sure God understands and forgives. But we still suffer the consequences of our dullness of hearing, because, although God understands and forgives, the law is still in operation.

This perhaps explains why bad things happen to good people. Many times it is simply because they have brought those things upon themselves by their ignorance of God's laws.

If you or I accidentally step off the edge of a cliff, God will understand and forgive our honest mistake. But we are still going to fall, because of the law of gravity. Then people will wonder why the Lord "allowed such a terrible thing to happen to such a godly person." God really had nothing to do with it. Our fall was a direct result of our own negligence. That's why we need to know the spiritual laws that govern this universe as well as we know the physical laws by which it operates.

Many times we don't understand why God doesn't do this or that or the other thing for us. While we ourselves are totally ignorant of the laws that bring about the thing we want to see done in our life. And much of the time, the reason we are ignorant is because we are dull of hearing.

We wonder why we can't see ourselves healed, or prospering financially, or successful, or in a better job, or having a happy home. Often it is simply because of what we are hearing. *You cannot listen to garbage and see a garden!* What you hear is what you will see. And what you see is what you will get — what you will ultimately wind up doing.

Is there still rebellion in you, animosity, fear, frustration? Where do you suppose all that comes from? Not from God, of course. It comes from the enemy, from Satan. But how does it get into you, into your system, into your inmost being? Through your ears! You have been allowing the law of hearing to work against you.

Like Cookie, you need a better image of your God. (She has that image now.) You need to see Him as a loving Father. That is why Jesus came to this earth: to reveal God as He really is, to give us a true image of our heavenly Father as one who loves and cares for His dear children.

Jesus came to this earth for you and me! He came to open our eyes to see God as an almighty, all-powerful, all-loving Father who delights in doing good to His children — One who will feed us, take care of us, bless us. That's the image of your Father that you need to get engraved in your mind and heart.

But it won't happen automatically. You have to work at it. You have to constantly hear these things and receive them into your mind and spirit. And you also have to reject whatever you hear that doesn't conform to that image.

You see, Satan knows this law and how it works as well as you and I do. He knows how to use it for his advantage. That's why it is so important that we Christians learn how to use it *against* the devil and *for* ourselves and others around us. We need to be speaking the Word *against* Satan and *for* ourselves!

If you know how, you can turn this law around and make it work for you rather than against you. You can refuse to listen to the enemy and instead tune in on some Good News—the Word of God. Read what He has to say about you. Change your perspective. Find a church that preaches the love of God—not condemnation. Fill your mind and heart with good things, good images, good thoughts. . . . **if there be any virtue, and if there be any praise, think on these things!** (Phil. 4:8)

You need to reprogram your mind just like reprogramming a computer. Remember, your mind can only compute what you input. So be careful what you allow into your memory bank!

Turn that law around. Make it work for you. Make it produce blessings, dividends, and benefits in your life. The choice is yours. Don't be dull of hearing.

8
Be Careful How You Hear

> Take heed therefore how ye hear: for whosoever hath, to him shall be given; and whosoever hath not, from him shall be taken even that which he seemeth to have.
> Luke 8:18

What you hear is content.

How you hear is attitude.

In Luke 8:18, Jesus is dealing with a basic principle. He is not just dealing with the content of the law of hearing, but also with the attitude. Did you know that your attitude affects your hearing? So attitude becomes an important part of understanding the law of how we are able to retain things — the law contained in Luke 8:18.

Stanford University ran a survey one time and found that to change an opinion a person has to hear something eleven times to eradicate the old opinion and seven more times to establish the new one.

You would have to hear something a minimum of eighteen times in order to change your opinion. But if you don't have the right attitude when you hear something, your opinion still won't change. So you see that how you hear becomes a major factor in life.

One time an older couple who had been married twenty-five or thirty years came in for counseling. I said, "All right, what can I do to help you?"

They kind of looked at each other. Neither one of them spoke.

Finally, I said, "Well, one of you speak up."

They looked at each other again, then she burst out crying: "It's him! It's him! He doesn't love me anymore!"

He said, "I do too. I told you last week that I loved you."

She said, "No, you don't! I heard how you said it."

It wasn't what she heard. It was how she heard it.

When your attitude is affected, you see things that aren't there and miss things that were there. What you hear and how you hear it — the attitude you hear it with — can either build or destroy. If you can get hold of this in your life and watch your attitude when you hear, it will make the difference. In my own life I watched how this law of hearing almost destroyed my church.

When I first started the church, the blessings began to flow. Healings, manifestations, financial miracles, all kinds of things transpired. We were being blessed by God, and people were saying this was the greatest church they'd ever been in. They were saying I was the greatest pastor. They were saying I was teaching truths they'd never heard before. It was exciting, wonderful! There was a surge of God's power, and God blessed us to such a great degree because the people had such a good attitude and were so excited about the church.

They were excited about what they were hearing.

The church took off and in two years' time grew from 165 to 2,200 members.

You think, "Oh, that's wonderful!"

But then the Lord told me to go to the north part of Tulsa because that's where the need was. I obeyed God and moved there. Six weeks later, I looked up and I had 600 people left. Great concern rose up in me. I was concerned not only about where I was financially, but about what I had done wrong.

Had I missed God? Did I know the voice of God? I was at the point of even asking myself if I knew God.

At first, I couldn't peg what was wrong. Then the Lord dealt with me, and I began to really hear what people were saying. They had begun to change what they were saying. They began to say, "He's missed God," "The Spirit of God has departed," "Icabod is written over the church."

As a result, things started going down. That wasn't the only reason the church started going down. But this law helped to carry it, because the law of hearing had become perverted. As a result, no matter what I said, people didn't hear what I was actually saying.

It wasn't just what they were hearing — and it took a while for me to spot that. As we read before, Luke 8:18 says, **Take heed therefore how ye hear: for whosoever hath, to him shall be given; and whosoever hath not, from him shall be taken even that which he seemeth to have.**

When you tie that in with Mark 4:3-32, the parable of the sower, you begin to realize what Jesus is saying. You begin to see another part of this law, that without the proper hearing — without the right attitude — you wind up with the wrong picture.

Words paint pictures. The Word creates the vision. The Word gives you the hope. But what you're hearing and how you hear it affects the picture you get. I know that if I don't keep my attitude right, even when somebody says something good to me, I won't hear it right. My wife can say something to me to try to help me, but if my attitude isn't right, I'll receive it as criticism.

I'm not able to hear her properly because of my attitude, and then we'll get into a fuss. When we're at the point of dissention and confusion, strife will set in. Then we'll have to turn right around and get forgiveness and start all over. All because of my wrong attitude.

Just Do It

And I'm not the only one who's ever felt this way. All of us do this.

When I began to see this principle, I began to see what God was trying to bring me into, and what all this could mean. I began to see what Jesus meant in Mark 4:24,25: **Take heed what ye hear: with what measure ye mete, it shall be measured to you: and unto you that hear shall more be given. For he that hath, to him shall be given: and he that hath not, from him shall be taken even that which he hath.**

I didn't understand a certain part of this law until God began to give me revelation after I got discouraged with the church going down. Two types of people began to affect me. One group of people would quit coming to church. They were just no longer there. The devil would jump on the bandwagon, beat me over the head, and say, "See — you're not a good pastor. You don't even feed the people." And I would get real low.

The other group of people would come and be kind and gracious to me. They would say, "Oh, Pastor, we love you and consider you to be a man of God. But you just don't feed us anymore. So we're going to have to go over to Brother So-and-So's church. He's a great teacher, and he'll be a great blessing to us. Therefore, we're going over there to get fed."

Because I loved the sheep and wanted them to grow, I wanted them to go where they were going to get fed. They are God's sheep. As a pastor, I am just the under-shepherd. But I have a responsibility to feed and take care of the people God has entrusted me with. So I would get even more despondent and down, hearing that the sheep entrusted to me were not getting fed.

One day the Spirit of the Lord said to me, "Go back and listen to your own tapes."

Be Careful How You Hear

I thought, "No, I don't want to do that. I don't even like the sound of my own voice."

But the Lord kept dealing with me and saying, "Go back and listen to your own tapes."

So finally I gave in and went back and started listening. As I listened to the truth that I was preaching I thought, "Hey, that's good stuff. I didn't know I knew that!" Then I thought, "Man, you can live on that! You can grow and develop on that. What on earth is going on here?"

All of a sudden the Lord began to teach me about how you hear. Mark 4:24 says, . . . **for he that hath, to him shall be given.**

All of a sudden I saw it.

"He that hath" what?

A good attitude!

To him shall be given.

Individuals can open themselves up to the revelation of God, and by their attitudes, can determine how much revelation they will get. If they have a good attitude, not only will they get what the man of God is saying, they'll also get what the Spirit of God is saying. And that's what it's all about. I really don't care whether anybody hears me or not. I want people to hear what God is saying.

I'm anointed of God and called of God and what I have to say is naturally going to have some value to it. But if people don't have the right attitude, they won't hear me. And if they don't hear me, then they can't hear God in what I'm saying.

So I began to see — he that hath a good attitude, to him shall be given.

Did you ever notice how men of God when they're preaching will go down little side paths and trails and deal with totally different subjects, then go back again to the main area they're teaching? That's because some person walked into the service with a good attitude, looking for answers, searching for truths, and the Spirit of God just led that man right over there to deal with that subject. This happens because God wants to meet the needs of His people. With a good attitude, you'll pull out revelation. You'll pull out answers. You'll bring forth the best of God when you keep a good attitude in your hearing.

Come with expectancy. God won't fail you. Come to Him in faith and with that expectancy.

But there's also a negative side to this law. I don't explain this to scare you — I simply want you to understand the operation of the law. The rest of the verse says, **For he that hath** (a good attitude)**, to him shall be given; and he that hath not . . .** (Hath not what? A good attitude.) **. . . from him shall be taken even that which he hath.**

There's the danger. That's what happened to those two types of people in my church.

One young lady in my church had been a prostitute out on the streets before our people went out there and won her to the Lord. She came to church, got filled with the Spirit, and was really turned on to God. We helped her get into business. All kinds of good things began to break forth in her life for a couple of years. But I noticed she was struggling at times, then finally, she quit coming to church.

I sent one of the assistant pastors out to check on her. He discovered that she was back on the streets again. I couldn't understand. How could someone who had the kind of revelation that we have turn around and go the other way? How could someone turn around and go back into a life of prostitution after living for God, knowing His righteousness and grace, His power and mercy? Doing that is like what Proverbs 26:11 talks about — a dog returning to his own vomit. How could someone partake of the same way of life all over again?

Then I saw the revelation.

When that young lady developed a bad attitude toward the church, toward the people and toward me, she began not to hear me. As a result, she cut herself off from the revelation of God. You're either walking toward the light or away from it. You're either moving in revelation or away from revelation. I began to see what had happened to her. That also helped me understand "he that hath not, hath not what?" A good attitude. **From him shall be taken, even that which he hath.**

Not only did she lose out on what I was teaching at the time, but because of the law of how you hear, she began to go farther away. She lost all the revelation that she had.

If you continue to go to church with the wrong attitude, you'll not only miss what the man of God is saying, you'll miss what the Spirit of God is saying, too. You'll start to lose the revelation you got last week. If you keep on going, you'll lose what you had the week before that. Keep going, and you'll lose what you had the week before that until you can backslide while sitting right there in the church pew. How dangerous it is to come to church with the wrong attitude!

What attitude should I go to church with? I should go to church with this attitude: This man of God is going to be anointed today. He's going to speak revelation of truth into my life. I'm not going to hear just what he says — I'm going to hear what the Spirit is saying. I'm going to have all my questions answered. I'm going to have understanding. God is going to bless and direct my path.

When you come with that attitude, revelation will explode inside you, all because you made a quality decision to be careful how you hear.

If you don't hear right, you don't see right. That's what I saw about the people who said I didn't feed them anymore. Their attitudes had changed and, as a result, because they had a good attitude toward someone else, they were ready to move on. There are what we call "cruise-a-matics," people who float in and out, just because their attitudes have become affected to the point that they can't hear God properly.

We've got to hear the right things being said by the right people. That's the content. But we've got to have our attitudes right to make sure we hear what was said. How we hear affects the reality of what we hear. How we hear changes our lives. God, help us to control our attitudes so that we can be in the place we need to be to hear, through the people God's wanted to put in our lives, what the Spirit of God wants to say to us.

9
Cause People to Hear Joy

A number of years ago I worked for a ministry leading the song services in their meetings. During this time an elderly couple used to attend the seminars and seemed to enjoy hearing me sing "Amazing Grace." The man, realizing he was up in years and close to death, told his wife, "When I go on to be with the Lord, I want you to have Buddy Harrison sing 'Amazing Grace' at my funeral." So his wife agreed.

When the man died, sure enough, His wife called me and asked if I would sing at the funeral. Of course, I said I would. As it turned out, the funeral was to be held in a denominational church. Before going to the service, I spent considerable time in prayer, preparing my heart to minister life to the lady and those in attendance.

Since my song was to be at the end of the service, I sat on the platform waiting for my turn to participate. There were other songs to be presented, then two ministers were to speak.

The first minister got up and started talking. His message was so filled with death, doubt, and unbelief it was almost unbearable. Of course, the poor widow was already in tears because of her deep grief. After all, she had been married to this man for almost 50 years. Naturally there was bound to be a keen sense of loss.

It was obvious she was already struggling to deal with the situation, and this insensitive preacher, with his gloom and despair, wasn't helping matters in the least. His manner and remarks were so heartless, it wasn't long before the poor woman was sobbing bitterly. She was bent over with grief and pain. Still the man didn't let up a bit.

Seeing the lady like that was just tearing me up inside. I was hurting so badly for her that I was in agony. I prayed silently, "Oh, Lord, this is not right. This minister is hurting this poor woman. He's tearing her up inside with his words. Father, You have got to do something. I can't stand this."

So I gritted my teeth and suffered through the first message. But then the second minister got up, and he was worse than the first! In fact, he went so far as to tell the widow that it wouldn't be long before she would be going on to join her dead husband.

By this time the poor woman was sobbing so badly she could hardly get her breath. In my mind and heart I could literally see her dying by degrees. I wasn't at all sure she was going to make it through that service (or me either, for that matter!) because of the death that was being poured out by the words being spoken.

It was evident to me that the agony the speaker was laying on that woman was building moment by moment. Finally it began to mushroom beyond control. Inside, I ached for her. Tears were overflowing my eyes despite everything I could do to hold them back.

In anguish I cried out inside, "Oh, Lord! You've got to do something! I can't take this. This poor woman is being tormented to death, and I am powerless to stop it. I can't get up and publicly rebuke these two ministers of the gospel right here in their own church. I don't have that kind of authority. I haven't been in the ministry long enough to even consider such a thing. Lord, *You've* got to do something!"

Finally the man finished his remarks and sat down. It was time for me to sing. I got to my feet and moved forward to the microphone. I took a deep breath and opened my mouth to sing. Only it didn't come out in English. I started to sing in tongues!

I knew from the way those eyeballs were rolling that I was in trouble. It was obvious right away that this was not the norm for that church. Yet it was not premeditated on my part. I would never have had the audacity to even plan such a thing, much less carry it out. It just happened. I just opened my mouth, and it jumped out. It rose up from down on the inside of me and before I had time to think of what was happening, it had happened.

I was as shocked as the congregation. All of a sudden, without the slightest warning or provocation, here I was standing up at a funeral in a strange church singing in tongues to the tune of "Amazing Grace"! I can assure you that was not my idea!

I finished that verse and then sang the interpretation. As I was singing, I noticed out of the corner of my eye that the widow had quit sobbing. She had lifted her head and was looking at me. She was still crying, but was more in control of herself.

I sang another verse in tongues. Then I sang the interpretation. By the time I had finished that verse, the lady still had tears in her eyes, but she wasn't crying anymore.

Suddenly I sensed something happen inside me. Following the leading I was feeling, I changed tempos and went into one of those foot-stomping, hand-clapping type rhythms. And I started singing that tune in tongues. I knew I was in trouble already, so this time I just closed my eyes and forgot that anybody was there except the Lord and that poor grief-striken widow.

I began singing the interpretation of that song to that dear lady and the essence of it was that her husband had gone on to be with the Lord. That he was up there right at that very moment, filled with heavenly delight and joy, dancing before the throne in the presence of the Most High God.

As I was singing, I opened my eyes and looked down. The widow was dancing in the aisle!

What a transformation! An atmosphere that a few minutes before had been laden with death, despair and defeat was now charged with life and hope and victory! All because of one divine law: What you hear is what you see, and what you see is what you will do.

What had caused the difference? Words. That widow just determined within herself, "If my husband is dancing before the Lord right now, I might as well join him." And so she did. She danced at her husband's funeral. And they both enjoyed it.

Later on, after that experience, I began to reflect upon it. I thought about it a great deal. Have you ever done something which you knew in your heart was right, but you couldn't think of a scripture to cover it?

In my heart I knew I had followed the Spirit of the Lord because what I had done wasn't premeditated. It had just come up out of my spirit spontaneously. I *knew* it was right. But for the life of me I couldn't think of a scripture to justify what I had done.

So I began to look in the Word. For three weeks I searched the scriptures. Finally I found a verse that became *rhema* to me. Now I realize this verse has other applications, but at that time God used it to speak to my heart concerning what I had done. The verse is Psalm 51:8: **Make me to hear joy....**

I saw it instantly. The Spirit of the Lord had used me to cause that lady to hear joy. Why? Because the joy of the Lord is our strength. (Neh. 8:10.) God had wanted to strengthen her at the time of her greatest need. So He had used me to speak forth that word of joy that changed her whole outlook and gave her a new hope and a new determination.

God wants to use all of us that way. My prayer for you is that for the rest of your life God will cause you to hear joy and to speak joy. I pray that you never again hear or speak death, doubt, unbelief, or defeat. I pray God that you guard your ears and your mouth, that you never allow anyone to put any negativism on you and that you refuse to put it on anyone else. I pray that you take the law of hearing and make it work for you and for all those who come in contact with you.

You see, that law is going to work on you for the rest of your life whether you want it to or not, whether you realize it or not. So you might as well make up your mind right now to make it work the right way: for good. It has been in operation all this time. That's why you're where you are at this moment.

If you don't like where you are now, change your situation and circumstance with this law. You don't have to stay where you are or the way you are. You can go onward and upward. The Bible teaches that we are to go on **from glory to glory** (2 Cor. 3:18). It is God's ultimate plan for you that you go from glory to glory, to glory to glory, right straight into Glory!

God *wants* you to work this law in your life. He desires the very best for you: health, prosperity, success, freedom, peace, power, joy. Take this law and use it to bring happiness to yourself and to others. Make people to hear joy.

10
Catch the Vision

Proverbs 29:18 tells us, **Where there is no vision, the people perish...** If you don't have a vision, you too will "perish." You will never do anything of lasting significance for God. But if you ever do get a vision, it will be produced by what you hear. Hearing is what causes you to see.

In November of 1977, the Lord spoke to me. My wife and I were in Saginaw, Michigan, for a meeting. One night at the hotel we were listening to the tape, "Can We Go Past Pentecost?" by Ralph Mahoney. The Lord began dealing so powerfully with my heart that I couldn't stand it. I jumped out of bed, knelt at the foot of the other bed, and began crying out to God and praying in the Spirit.

Suddenly I heard the voice of God say to me, "Now go back to Tulsa and start a family church, charismatic teaching center and reach the world for Me." Instantly I received a vision of that church. Today that vision has become reality. But from the very beginning when I received that vision, I saw ours as a balanced church. I saw it as a family church, a charismatic teaching center, and a world outreach — all of these things.

You see, that is where many people miss it. They don't get the whole picture, the full image. They only see part of what God has in mind for them.

Some churches are nearsighted. All they can see is themselves. That's all they care about. They seem to care nothing about the people across town or across the seas.

Just Do It

They are like the old farmer who prayed, "Lord, bless me, my wife, my son John, and his wife—us four, no more!" That is why they develop these little "bless me" clubs. They get together and say in essence, "You prophesy to me, brother, then I'll prophesy to you." That's the only vision they have. They are nearsighted.

And then there are those who are farsighted. They only see how wonderful it is going to be "when we all get to heaven." They get together and sing and preach about how "over in Glory we will not shed a tear." All they seem to be interested in is "the sweet by and by."

Why? Because all they have ever heard about is heaven. Therefore, that's all they know. They can't tell you what is happening here and now because they don't know. They don't even know there is revival going on, that the Spirit of God is being poured out and is moving in a mighty way right now. All they see is, "Somehow, someway, some day I'll get to Glory." They are farsighted.

God wants His Church to have 20/20 vision. He wants us to be able to see near and far, today and tomorrow, the here and now as well as the hereafter — normal vision.

That is what we have in our church in Tulsa. We see that we are a family church to meet the needs of our local body of believers, a charismatic teaching center to minister to those around us, and a world outreach center to carry the Gospel to the whole world. God wants us to see all those spheres and not be limited to just one.

Some churches think only of missions. That is all they've got going. If they didn't have missions, they wouldn't have any reason to exist. Thank God for missions. Let's not get down on missions just because some people carry them to excess. But let's also not go to the other extreme and get so self-centered we put ourselves back in a hole so all we think of is ourselves and our little group. We need a balanced view of our place and role as members of the Body of Christ.

Have you ever heard Christians say something like this? "Oh, we can't afford to let our young people go over to that other church, we might lose them." My answer to that is, "If you take care of them, you won't lose them."

There shouldn't be any fear in fellowship. We Christians need to learn to recognize that we are one in Christ, one in Spirit, one in faith. But as Paul points out in 1 Corinthians 12:12, though we are one Body we are all different parts of that Body. Therefore, we are not all alike. Unity does not mean uniformity.

Churches are different just as people are different, because churches are made up of people — individuals with individual personalities and viewpoints. Our philosophy ought to be: If people can get helped better over in another church, then we have an obligation to send them over there. As Christians, our first consideration ought to be the welfare of others, not building an institution. We should love people enough to desire what is best for them, then let them decide that for themselves.

But some church people seem to have a hard time seeing it that way. Many believers are what I call "owl Christians." You know how an owl is. The more light that comes in, the less he sees. What does an owl do during the day while the rest of us are active, walking in the light, taking advantage of the glorious life that is ours? He sits out on a limb by himself with his eyes closed, shutting out everything, doing nothing.

We dare not allow ourselves to become "owls." We must keep our eyes and our minds open. We must have a vision. Where does the vision come from? From what we hear.

Let me illustrate both sides of this concept from my own experience. One time I was playing offensive guard on our high school football team. We were going down to Beaumont, Texas, to play another team and I had to play opposite a linesman who was six-foot-five and weighed 265 pounds! At that time I stood about five-feet-eleven and weighed in at a whopping 154 pounds! Can you imagine what was going through my mind at the prospect of having to try to overrun that bulldozer? I was petrified.

But fortunately my coach knew something about the law of hearing. He started getting me prepared just as my basketball coach had done to prepare me to face that giant redwood. He started filling my head with positive images. He began telling me: "Harrison, you can do it. This guy's big, but he's slow. Real slow. If you will just get the first lick in real hard, you'll tear him up. Then you'll have the upper hand the whole game." So all week long he kept drilling one thought into my brain: "You can take him, Harrison, you can take him."

In the sports world this is known as getting someone "psyched up." It is supposed to be purely psychological, which it can be. But it doesn't have to be.

You can take the Word of God and "psyche yourself up" to whip the devil, because it is a spiritual law that what your mind sees, your body tends to perform.

Isn't that "mind science," mind over matter? No, it's *spirit* over matter. There is a difference. The Word of God is spirit. (John 6:63; Heb. 4:12.) And once spoken forth in faith, that Word produces an effect. It will not return void, without having accomplished that to which it was sent. (Is. 55:11.)

But before the Word can affect your spirit, it must first penetrate and affect your mind. That's why you need to hear it over and over until you get the picture.

Catch the Vision

The coach kept telling me that I could take that big bruiser. I watched the game films on him and, sure enough, he was slow. I watched him when we went out on the practice field that day. Whenever the other team called signals, this fellow was always about a half a count behind the rest of the line. Because he was so big, he was clumsy. I knew then that I had the jump on him.

When we lined up opposite each other the first time, he looked like a big tree. I thought to myself, "If this guy falls on me, I'll be crushed." But I had made up my mind that I was going to hit him so hard and so fast he wouldn't know what hit him. I was ready. I got set, dug in, and waited for the signal. When the ball was hiked, I fired out of my position like a shot. I hit that linesman with everything I had, catching him just as he was raising up. I went in low and that guy turned a complete flip.

During the rest of the game that big gorilla literally ran from me! Why? Because what I had heard had produced a picture in me. What I saw, I did. I had caught the vision!

Now let's take a look at this on the negative side. On another occasion we played against a team from Baytown, Texas, which later went on to win the state championship. The linebacker I was to block on this team wasn't quite as big as the other boy. He was about six feet-one and weighed about 225 pounds. But he was quick and strong. Everyone told me, "This guy is so fast and powerful if you don't watch out he's going to eat your lunch!" They told me that. I heard that. I saw it that way. And that's exactly the way it turned out!

What you hear will cause you to see it that way, and ultimately it will be that way. "What you have heard and seen in me, do." Since faith comes by hearing, and hearing by the Word of God, then hearing the Word of God will produce an image down inside of us until we see ourselves victorious, triumphant, winning, free of fear, prosperous, and in possession of abundant and everlasting life.

God has assured us throughout His Word that it is His desire to give us the very desires of our heart. When that Word comes into our ears, it paints a picture of that promise on our minds and hearts. We begin to actually see ourselves in possession of the things we most desire. Whatever we receive from God materially, we must first receive mentally and spiritually. That's how the Word of faith operates. First you hear it, then you see it, then you have it.

In Mark 11:24 the Lord Jesus said: **What things soever ye desire, when ye pray, believe that ye receive them, and ye *shall* have them.** Notice that He said nothing about what to do if we do not pray. Do we fail to receive? Fail to succeed? Fail to win? What stops us? What we have heard causes us to see ourselves as a failure.

We program failure into ourselves, even into our own children. We tell them over and over how worthless they are, how stupid, how lazy, how incapable. Then we wonder why they end up worthless, stupid, lazy and incapable. By our own words in the past we have negatively programmed our own mates, our own children, our own selves, because people—especially those closest to us—have a strong tendency to become what they see. And they see what they hear.

That's why we need to learn to reprogram our minds, change our way of thinking and speaking, and redirect our words. We need to start saying what God says about us and our loved ones rather than what the world and the enemy says about us and them.

There is an order here: Hear, see, do. When you face any difficult situation in life, there are three basic ways you can react. You can: 1) *resign* yourself to it, 2) *resent* it, or 3) *rejoice* in the midst of it. The choice is yours. Let me give you an example.

Brother Harley Bendenhoff tells about a fellow who fell all the way down a flight of stairs. How did he react? At the bottom, he got up, shook himself off, and said, "Whew, I'm glad that's over!" He chose to rejoice!

Some people tend to lay everything that happens to them off onto "fate." But the Bible says, **According to your faith be it unto you** (Matt. 9:29). Not according to your *fate*, or your *fortune*, or your *friends*, or your *family*, but according to your FAITH.

"But where do I get this faith?"

What does the Bible say? **So then faith cometh by hearing, and hearing by the word of God** (Rom. 10:17). When you hear the Word of God, you will see properly, have the right picture. The Word will paint that picture. It will produce an image inside you that will cause you to see things from God's point of view.

The Word of God is a mirror of how God sees you. Not how you see yourself, necessarily, or have seen yourself in the past: It's how God sees you. You need to renew your mind daily with the Word of God so you can see yourself the way God sees you: victorious, a winner, a conqueror, able to do all things through Christ who strengthens you, aware that you are not made for failure but for success.

When you hear the truth, that truth will set you free. Hearing the Word of God will give you a new perspective on life, a new image of yourself. You will begin to see yourself complete.

Did you know that you are complete? Now you may not feel like it, but you are. The Word of God says so: **For in him** (Christ) **dwelleth all the fulness of the Godhead bodily. And ye are complete in him, which is the head of all principality and power** (Col. 2:9,10). The Father, the Son, and the Holy Ghost all live in you. If that isn't enough power to put you over, then you'll never get over — you'll never make it.

But you will make it if you see yourself as God sees you. And the way to get God's view of you is to hear His Word and not just once.

If "faith cometh by hearing the Word of God," then it naturally follows that "faith goeth by not hearing the Word of God."

You say you don't have faith? It is because you are not hearing the Word. You have to get where the Word is preached. You have to avail yourself of a book or cassette tape or preacher or church — or all of these — from which you can feed continually on the Word of God. If what your church is preaching is not producing faith inside of you to be victorious and triumphant and a conqueror in life, then I suggest you change churches. Find one that does preach the Word.

"But I have seen so little of the vision, so little of what I am to do."

That is about to change. Right now the Word is causing a great stirring in your spirit. Tune in to that stirring within you and sooner or later it will be made very plain to you what to do. That which you are hearing through these written words is sounding in your inner ear.

You are now receiving new inspiration and new direction, a new vision and a new goal for your life. Begin to see yourself acting that out. Take the initiative. Act on what you see now, not on what you have seen in the past. Don't dwell on past failures and disappointments. The Lord says that there shall be no memory of former things. (Eccl. 1:11.)

For too many years, you have acted on somebody else's word. Purpose in your heart right this minute that from now on you are going to act solely upon the Word of God.

...Behold, *now* **is the accepted time; behold,** *now* **is the day of salvation** (2 Cor. 6:2). **...Lift up your head; for**

your redemption draweth nigh (Luke 21:28). Look up. Open your eyes. Catch the vision!

Books by Buddy Harrison

Understanding Authority for Effective Leadership

Getting in Position To Receive

Maintaining a Spirit-Filled Life

Just Do It

Count It All Joy
Eight Keys to Victory in
Times of Temptations, Tests, and Trials
Coauthored by Van Gale

The Force of Mercy
The Gift Before and Beyond Faith
Coauthored by Michael Landsman

Available from your local bookstore.

HARRISON HOUSE
P. O. Box 35035
Tulsa, OK 74153

Buddy Harrison is a man walking after love with an apostolic vision for what God is doing today. He moves in the gifts of the Spirit with sensitivity and understanding. He is Founder and President of Faith Christian Fellowship International Church, Inc. and Harrison House, Inc. in Tulsa, Oklahoma. He has authored several books.

As a small boy, Buddy was healed of paralyzing polio. More than 25 years ago he answered the call of God on his life. He is gifted vocally and began his ministry in music and the office of helps. He became Office Manager for Kenneth E. Hagin Ministries and for several years pioneered many areas as Administrator/Office Manager.

In November, 1977, the Lord instructed Buddy to start a family church, a Bible teaching center and a world outreach in Tulsa, Oklahoma. He has obeyed the Spirit of God whatever the cost. Through his obedience, Faith Christian Fellowship was born with 165 people in January, 1978. Now there are more than 373 FCF churches worldwide.

Buddy and his wife, Pat, are known around the world for their anointed teachings from the Word of God, and for their ability to communicate principles from the Word with a New Testament love. Buddy attributes any success he has to obeying the Spirit of God and living the Word.

While in Israel the Lord spoke to him to serve as Pastor to pastors and ministers. His goal is to aid ministers in the spiritual and in the natural. Ministers around the world have received blessings through Buddy's apostolic ministry since he obeyed the vision given in Israel. Under his direction, FCF has grown to become a lighthouse for other Word and Faith churches. Today over 1,250 ministers are affiliated/associated or licensed/ordained through FCF.

For a list of cassette tapes
by Buddy Harrison
or for other information,
write:

Buddy Harrison
P. O. Box 35443
Tulsa, OK 74153

Please include your prayer requests and comments when you write.

In Canada contact:

Word Alive
P. O. Box 284
Niverville, Manitoba
CANADA R0A 1E0

For international sales in Europe,
contact:

Harrison House Europe
Belruptstrasse 42 A
A — 6900 Bregenz
AUSTRIA

The Harrison House Vision

Proclaiming the truth and the power
Of the Gospel of Jesus Christ
With excellence;

Challenging Christians to
Live victoriously,
Grow spiritually,
Know God Intimately.